Inspired by
Dr. Morgan

Affirm Your Confidence

in 31 Days

Affirmations and Journals
to Start your day

Dr. Alberta Morgan
Copyright © 2023

Cover and interior design by Niokoba

Photos: Freepik.com

Dedication

I dedicate this book to my husband, my love,
my light and my Hero. Your endless love
helped me write this affirmation book.

To my sons and their wives, I pray
that your marriage is a reflection of
endearing love that lasts a lifetime.

To my four grandchildren, I pray that
each of you will accomplish your goals
and enjoy life to the fullest and while
you live never want for anything.

To all my clients past, present and future,
THANK YOU, for allowing me to serve you
it has been an awesome privilege.

Introduction

Self-confidence is the ability to believe that, no matter what is in front of you, you can accomplish it. A few examples are as follows: writing a research paper, showing up for a job interview, or researching information to buy a house and having positive expectations of a positive outcome.

I often remind clients that if there is lack of self confidant, it is important to work toward self-confidence. This can be accomplished through Talk Therapy, and other interventions. I believes that when people trust in their abilities, having confidence in themselves it could help alleviate stress and anxiety.

Having high levels of self-confidence, through self-care, affirmations, and interventions could help people achieve what they set out to do. When this happens people are able to maintain a steady sense of control over their lives. Self-confident people generally trust in their abilities, their power to say yes or no, and their judgment when faced with decisions.

I believe that repeating affirmations about your confidence will encourages your brain to process what you are saying and hopefully there will be a positive change. When you continuously affirm your confidence, and how important it is to you, your actions will hopefully have positive outcome of less, depression, stress and anxiety. I wholeheartedly believe this affirmation book could help everyone because life happens and sometimes it can leave you unsure about your career, your relationships, your self-worth. Your best is right in front of you!

Day 1

I have the right to
live life to the fullest,
and I will

Day 2

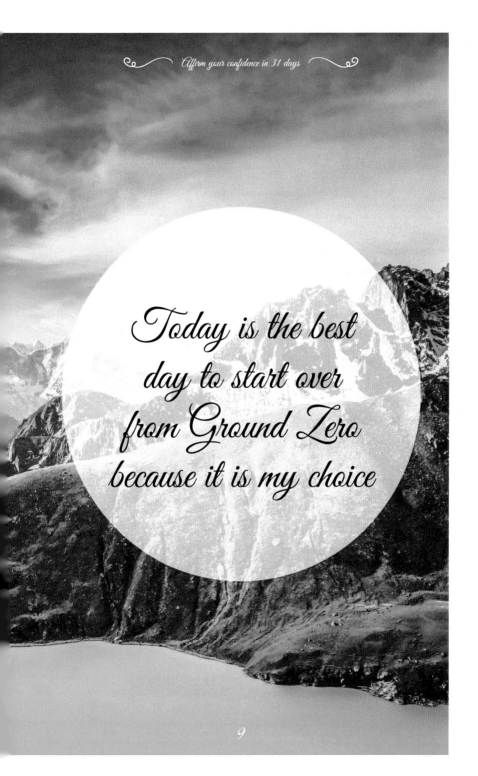

Today is the best
day to start over
from Ground Zero
because it is my choice

Day 3

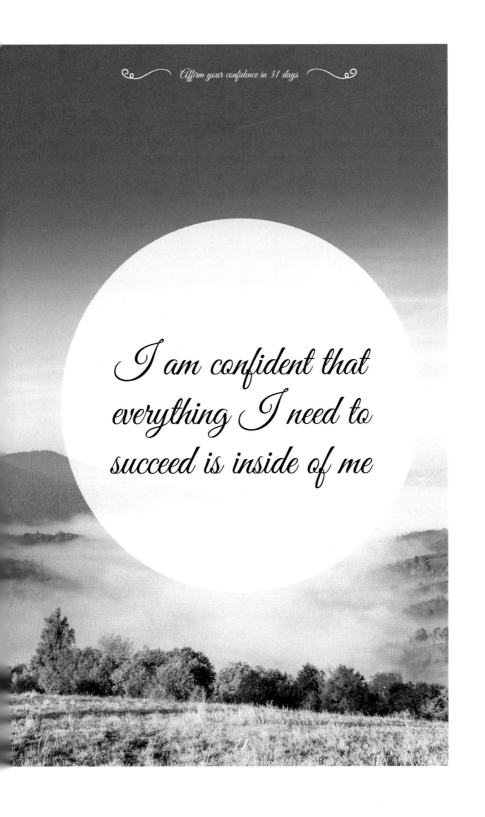

I am confident that everything I need to succeed is inside of me

Day 4

Whenever I am
in doubt, I need
to remember that
I am important

Day 5

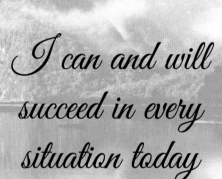

I can and will succeed in every situation today

Day 6

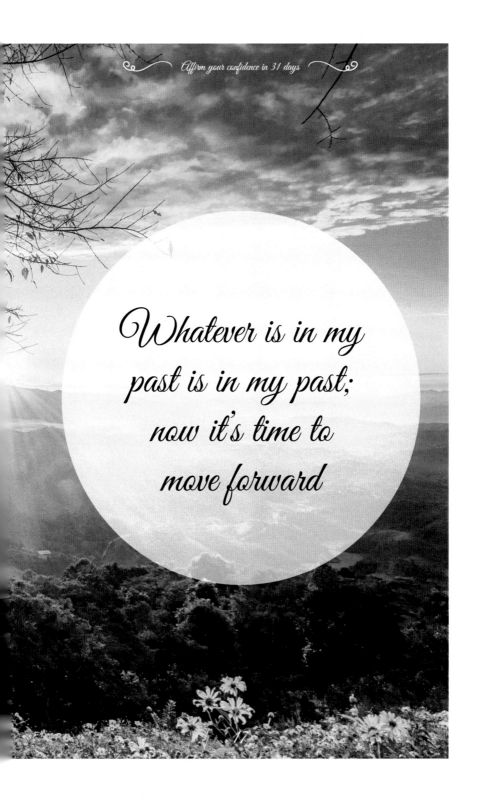

Whatever is in my past is in my past; now it's time to move forward

Day 7

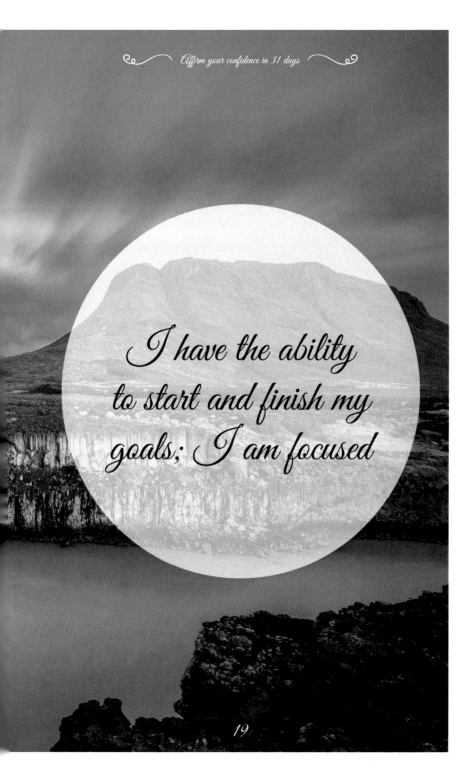

I have the ability
to start and finish my
goals; I am focused

Day 8

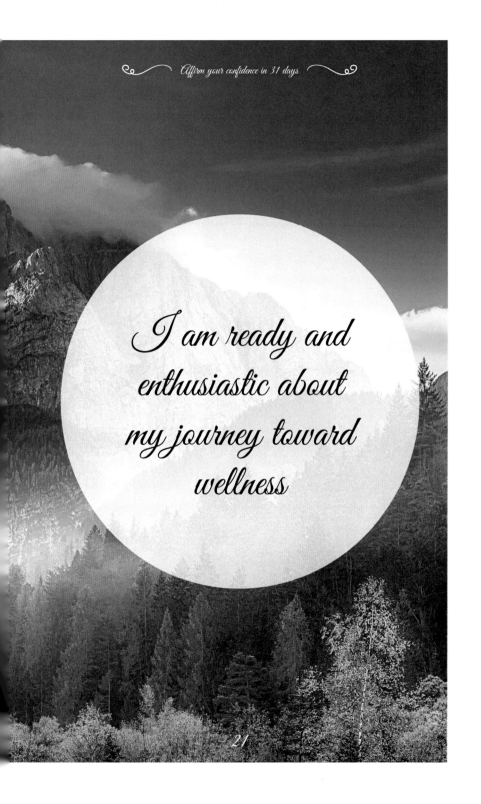

I am ready and enthusiastic about my journey toward wellness

Day 9

Every day I look forward to winning in body, mind, and spirit

Day 10

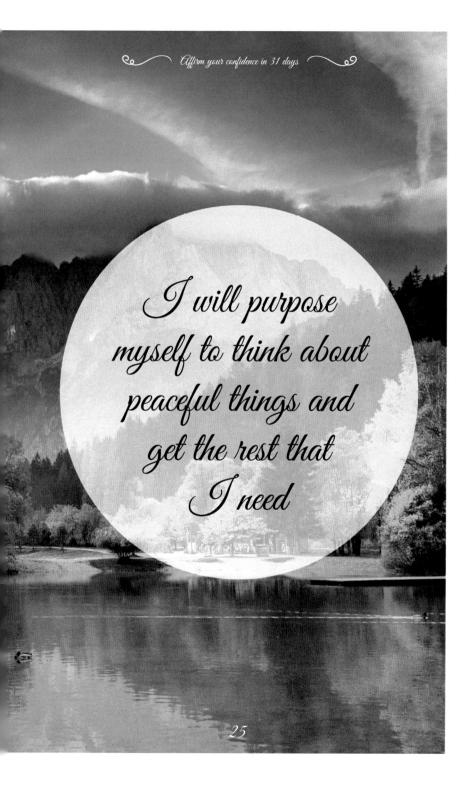

I will purpose myself to think about peaceful things and get the rest that I need

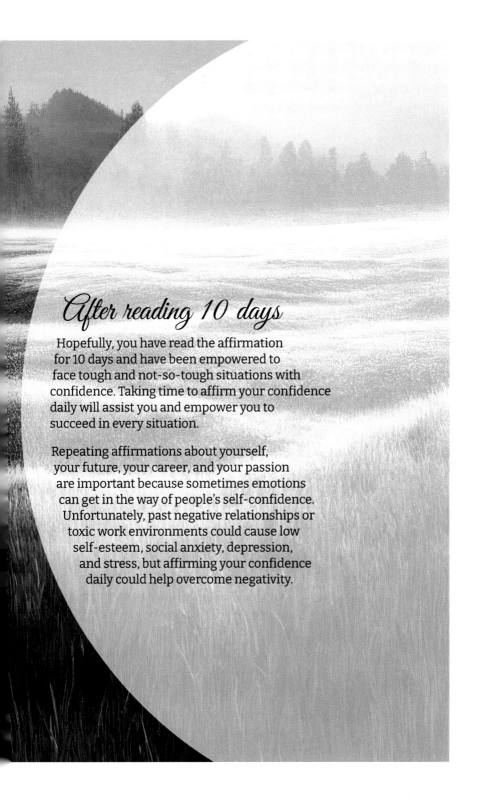

After reading 10 days

Hopefully, you have read the affirmation
for 10 days and have been empowered to
face tough and not-so-tough situations with
confidence. Taking time to affirm your confidence
daily will assist you and empower you to
succeed in every situation.

Repeating affirmations about yourself,
your future, your career, and your passion
are important because sometimes emotions
can get in the way of people's self-confidence.
Unfortunately, past negative relationships or
toxic work environments could cause low
self-esteem, social anxiety, depression,
and stress, but affirming your confidence
daily could help overcome negativity.

Day 11

I am confident that
things will work out
for my good everyday

Day 12

My well-being
includes taking time
for myself

Day 13

I am in love with myself and will continuously monitor my health and wellness

Day 14

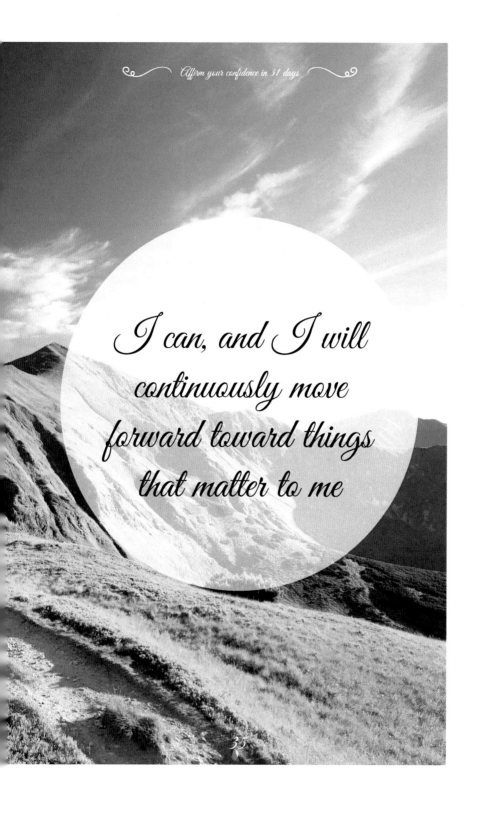

I can, and I will continuously move forward toward things that matter to me

Day 15

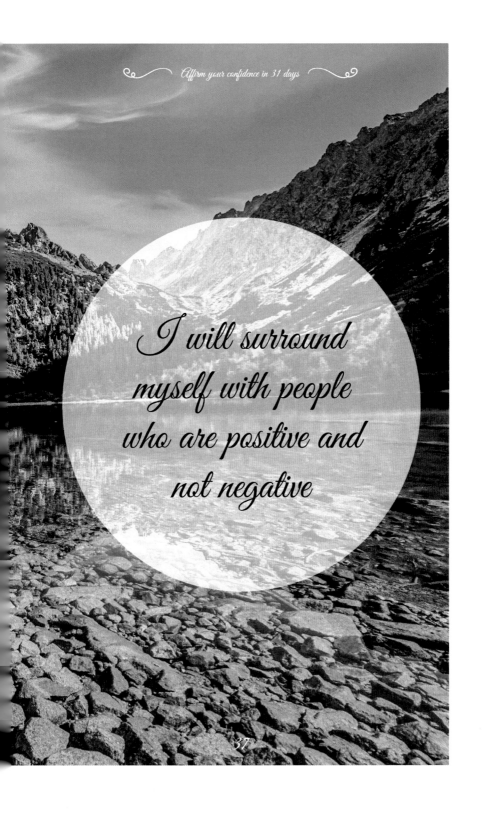

I will surround myself with people who are positive and not negative

Day 16

I can ask for help
if I am overwhelmed
and stressed

Day 17

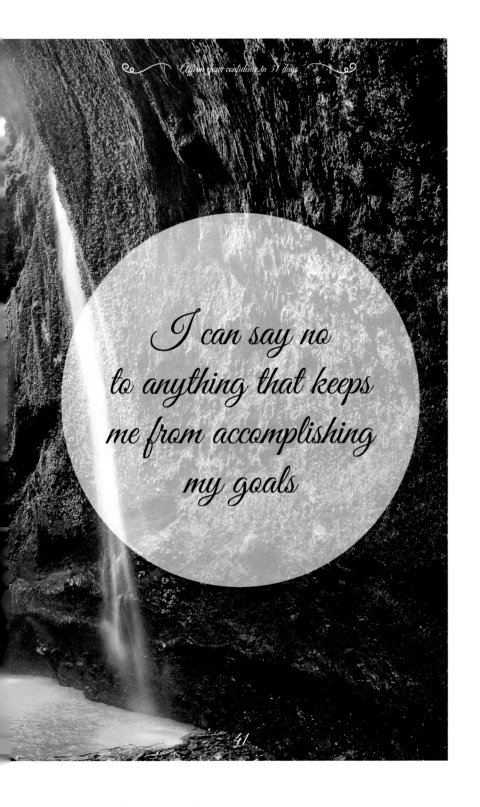

I can say no
to anything that keeps
me from accomplishing
my goals

Day 18

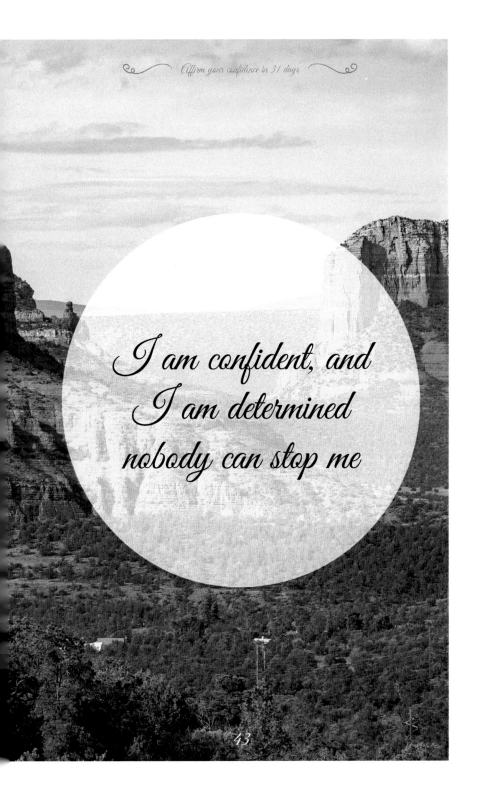

I am confident, and
I am determined
nobody can stop me

Day 19

I have the right
to choose what makes
me happy

45

Day 20

I am a wonderful person who has an amazing future ahead

After reading 20 days

After 20 days of taking time to read and think
about the affirmations, my hope for you is
that you will feel more confident and see
a positive change in your everyday life.

Being confident is accepting and trusting yourself
and having a sense of control in your life. People
are very aware of their strengths and weakness
and have positive or negative views about
themselves. Confident people are able to
set realistic goals and expectations, handle
criticism and communicate assertively.

Keep reading, you deserve to be empowered
and more focused on what matters to you.
You are amazing.

Day 21

I have the right
to take care of my
emotional well-being
before I take care
of others

Day 22

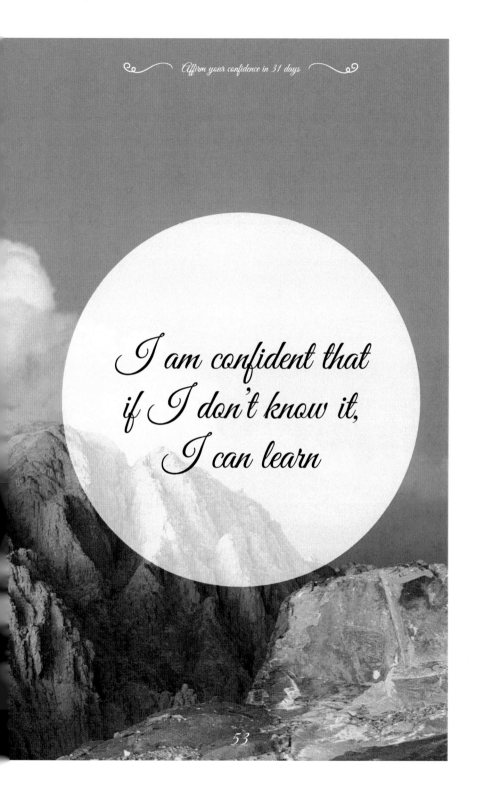

I am confident that
if I don't know it,
I can learn

Day 23

*Each day is
another opportunity
to be great*

Day 24

I will find and
look for opportunities
to meditate

Day 25

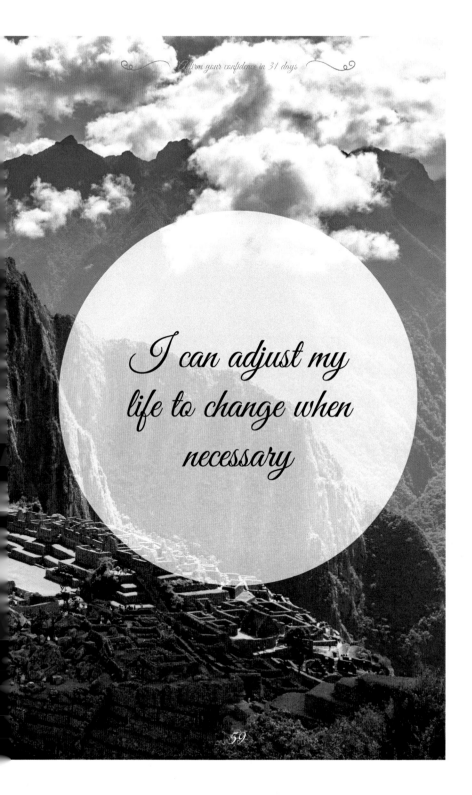

I can adjust my life to change when necessary

Day 26

I am confident that
I have a wonderful
future ahead of me

Day 27

I can ask for
help and not
feel ashamed

Day 28

*I can change my
mind to alleviate stress
and anxiety*

Day 29

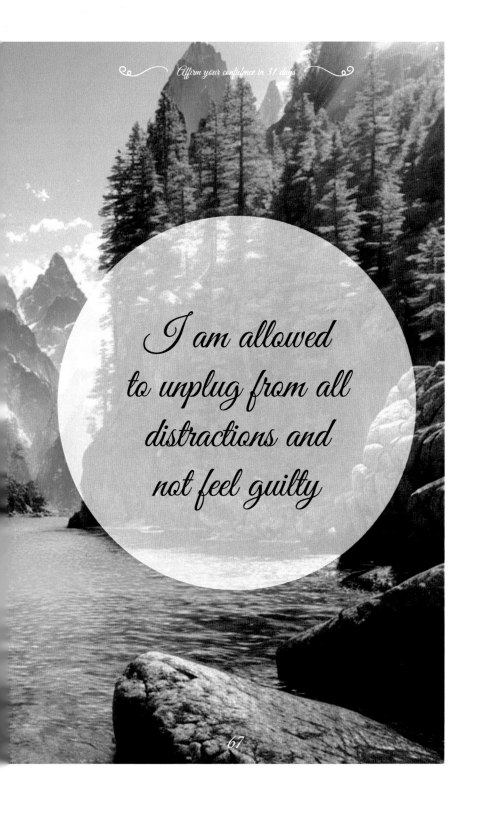

I am allowed
to unplug from all
distractions and
not feel guilty

Day 30

I have the
confidence, I can
and I will
WIN!

Day 31

I don't have limits;
I have freedom

31 days

After 31 days, if you have not already,
write down your thoughts in the journal
pages. Journaling can be incredibly beneficial for
your mental and physical health. I believe that it
could help boost your mood, allow you
to be creative, and overall make you happier.

Journaling could reduce your stress,
depression, and anxiety. When you journal,
it boosts your ability to cope with intrusive
and avoidant thoughts.

If you are unsure of what to journal about,
start by writing down how you feel and what you
need to accomplish in the next 5 days.

Stay focused, stay committed,
and be GREAT for you!

Dr. Morgan

Journal

Day 1

Day 2

Day 3

Day 4

Day 5

Day 6

Day 7

Day 8

Day 9

Day 10

Day 11

Day 12

Day 13

Day 14

Day 15

Day 16

Day 17

Day 18

Day 19

Day 20

Day 21

Day 22

Day 23

Day 24

Day 25

Day 26

Day 27

Day 28

Day 29

Day 30

Day 31

About the author

Dr. Alberta Morgan is the founder of Living Waters Counseling Center. She has more than 25 years of clinical experience as a psychotherapist and nearly 20 years of experience running a private practice.

Her clinical work focuses on helping people deal with depression, stress, anxiety, and other emotional problems through talk therapy, family and couples therapy, and cognitive behavioral therapy. Dr. Morgan is very passionate about helping people fulfill their goals and live their life to their fullest potential.

Her book of affirmations is life-changing and thought-provoking.

Dr. Morgan currently lives in New Jersey area with her husband and Havanese named Diamond.

107

Made in the USA
Columbia, SC
10 May 2023

1aab61ce-c5d6-403c-bf54-0f172a4ef598R05